Violent crime!

Learning Unlimited's
'Literacy for Active Citizenship' series

Written by Marylene Teixeira

GW00640857

Violent crime!
© Learning Unlimited 2018

Published by Learning Unlimited.

Foreword

Learning Unlimited's
'Literacy for Active Citizenship' series

The graded readers in the 'Literacy for Active Citizenship' series are primarily for adults who are settling in the UK, who are speakers of other languages (ESOL) and who are still developing their skills in English and in reading.

The first 20 titles in this series were produced as part of the EU-funded Active Citizenship and English (ACE) project (July 2013 – June 2015), led by Learning Unlimited. The ACE project supported migrant women to develop their skills and confidence in English and to take an active part in everyday life in the UK. We wanted to use the real-life experiences of our learners and volunteers in a writing strand of the project to support adult migrants settling in the UK. These stories, written by learners and volunteers, include funny, personal and less typical aspects of everyday life in the UK.

Additional titles in this series have also been written by learners and volunteers from Learning Unlimited's programmes. These include stories about more serious topics such as crime and health.

We hope you enjoy the 'Literacy for Active Citizenship' series. All the stories have been edited by ESOL specialists at Learning Unlimited. There are two versions of each story – Entry 1 (A1) and Entry 2+ (A2+), each with with free downloadable supporting materials: **www.learningunlimited.co/publications/esolreaders**

My name is Marylene. I was born
in Venezuela, a beautiful country in
South America.

My parents moved to Venezuela
from an island called Madeira.

They had five children and I was the
middle child.

Venezuela has lovely beaches and islands, high mountains, tropical forests and even a small desert. Venezuela has a lot of problems, too. In fact, it is one of the most violent countries in the world. I will tell you about some of the things that happened to me and why I left this beautiful country.

One day when I was 17 years old three men broke into our house. They had guns.

They took everything! They stole our money, our television, our kitchen equipment, our jewellery and our music system.

My father told the police what had
happened. A few days later the police
found my father's car. The seats, the
steering wheel and the battery were
all gone! The police did not arrest
anyone. My father said that the police
worked with the thieves.

A few years later I was on a bus on my way home from work. Two men got on the bus and they both had guns. I was really scared! They told the bus driver to lie down on the floor. One of men started driving the bus in a different direction. The other man stole all the passengers' bags and money. Then they stopped the bus and ran away.

I was very frightened. We were on the other side of the city in an area I did not know. I did not have any money. I phoned my father and he came to get me. We did not tell the police about this because they would not help.

After that I started to take a taxi home after work. Then one day another terrible thing happened. I was in a taxi on my way home. The driver said he had to take a different route because of an accident.

We arrived in a very poor area of the city. He stopped the car and took a gun from under his seat. He wanted to rape me.

I was very frightened and I started to cry. I said, "Don't you have a mother, a sister, a daughter or a niece?". I told him that I was young and not married yet.

He hit me with the gun and pushed
me out of the car. I looked at the back
of the car for a number plate but
there wasn't one. I had to take
another taxi to get home. I told my
sister about this taxi driver but I did
not tell my parents or the police.

After this, I decided I did not want to live in Venezuela any more. I went to live in Madeira.

The day I decided to leave, I felt sad because I knew I would never go back to Venezuela. It is too dangerous and there is too much violent crime!

A few years later, I got married.
Now I live with my husband and son
in London. I miss my family and my
friends and I miss the beauty of
Venezuela. I do not miss the violent
crime. In London, I feel safe.

Key words

crime	something that is illegal
dangerous	not safe
jewellery	things such as necklaces, rings, or bracelets that people wear for decoration
rape	force someone to have sex with you
niece	daughter of your sister or brother
number plate	a registration number on the front and back of a car
steal	take something from another person without permission
thief/ thieves	people who steal things from other people
tropical	from hot and humid areas near the Equator
violent	force to hurt or kill someone

Questions

1. Where do Marylene and her parents come from?

2. What are some of the good things about Venezuela?

3. What happened to Marylene and her family?

4. What did Marylene decide to do?

Talk in pairs:

5. Ask each other about some good things and problems in your home country or the country you live in now.

6. Marylene decided to stop reporting crimes to the police. Do you think this was the right decision? What do people do in your home country? Discuss this together.

Activity 1

Write a short story about your life. You can write about good things, bad things or both.

You can use Marylene's story to help you:

My name is ....

I am from ....

My parents are from ....

.... is a .... country.

It has ....

One day ....

Another day ....

A few years later ....

After .... years ....

Then ....

Now ....

Activity 2

Telling a story in the past

Marylene uses the simple past tense to tell her story. Can you remember the past simple for each of these irregular verbs? List your answers in a note book. Then find each of the verbs in the story and check if you were right. You can also check your answers with someone else:

1. break	7. hit
2. drive	8. miss
3. feel	9. say
4. get	10. steal
5. give	11. take
6. have	12. tell

Activity 3

Make a poster about your country.

You can use a map, postcards, photographs, labels and pictures from the internet.
Add some key information about your country to help other people find out more.
For example, you can add information about beautiful or important places and natural resources.

For more downloadable activities, visit:
www.learningunlimited.co/publications/esolreaders

Acknowledgements

Violent crime! was written by Marylene Teixeira.

Violent crime! was edited by Karen Dudley, Judy Kirsh, Julia McGerty and Foufou Savitzky at Learning Unlimited.

Images: Pixabay, p.1, 2, 3, 8,
Twenty20 Photos, p.4, 6,
Cover images: Pixabay and Twenty20 Photos

Designed by Daisy Dudley www.daisydudley.com